Home for the Holidays™

START A TRADITION

Solo Piano Arrangements
by Lorie Line

Edited by Anita Ruth

©1997 Time Line Productions, Inc.
222 Minnetonka Avenue South
Wayzata, MN 55391   (952) 474-1000

NOTES FROM THE ARTIST

Many of you have written to me, requesting more solo piano holiday arrangements. Thank you for all your requests. This year I decided to publish music from the entire album "Home For the Holidays." This is the best easy-listening music from my previously recorded "Sharing the Season" albums. And if you already have the accompanying sheet music for these three recordings, you'll be glad to know that this book has been revised and edited to be more "playable" for solo occasions. It also includes many new arrangements, not previously published.

Fans always ask me what gives me the most pleasure in what I do. The answer is definitely one thing… sharing with others what I love to create. And I hope you too, will be able to share this music with your family and friends during the holidays.

I hope you'll enjoy this book of music for many years to come. May it help to create happy memories for you.

Lorie Line

Full orchestrations of all Lorie Line music are available by special order for schools, churches, and ensembles. Each orchestration includes a conductor's score and separate parts. Call 1-800-801-5463 (LINE) for further information.

TABLE OF CONTENTS

I Saw Three Ships

Buoyantly

Arranged by Lorie Line

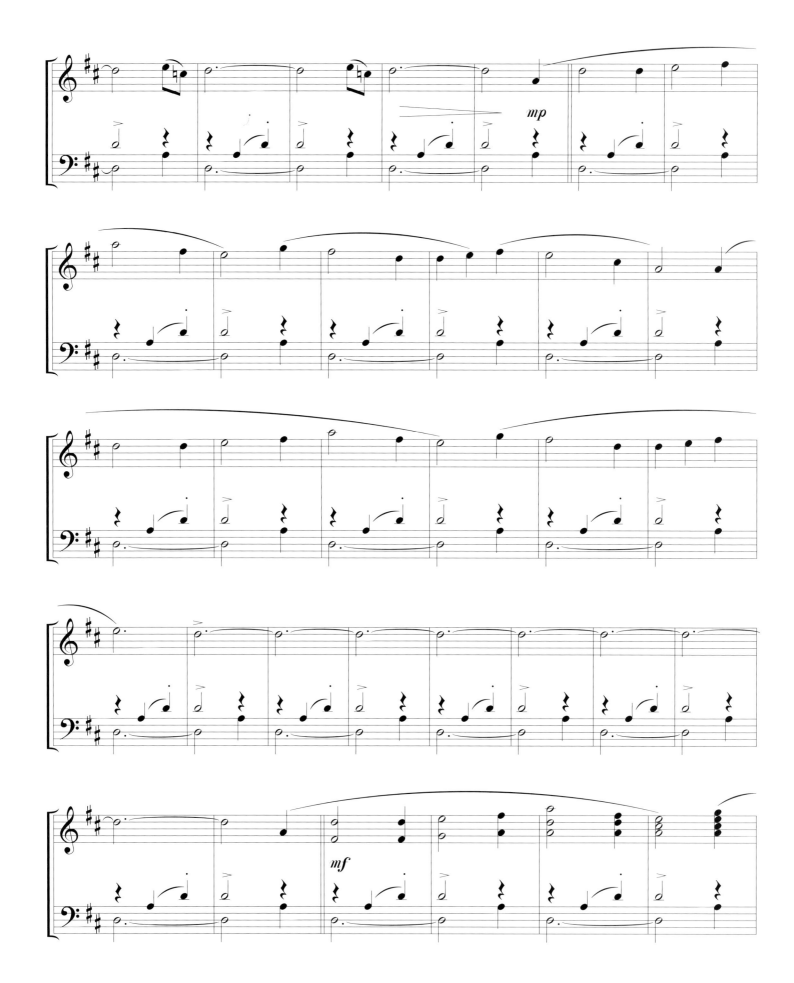

Sharply

mf

(Roll up)

Silent Night

Freely

Arranged by Lorie Line

A little more motion

O Come All Ye Faithful

Invitingly

Arranged by Lorie Line

With quiet hope

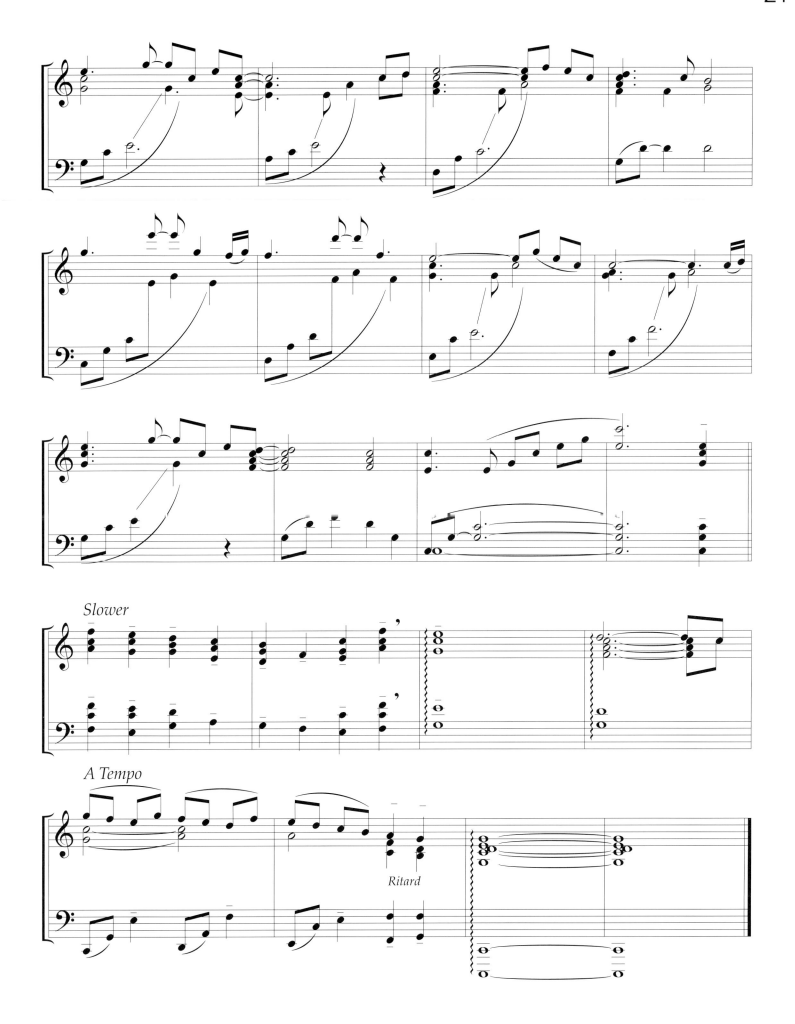

Joseph Dearest, Joseph Mine

Freely

Arranged by Lorie Line

Very Legato

We Three Kings

Joyfully dancing

Arranged by Lorie Line
*Revised from actual recording
for solo piano*

With spirit

Gesu Bambino

Sweetly, with childlike innocence

Arranged by Lorie Line

Away In A Manger

Simply

Arranged by Lorie Line

Once In Royal David's City

Dancing with anticipation

Arranged by Lorie Line

Freely

What Child Is This

With intent

Arranged by Lorie Line

The First Noel

Freely, with a clear pristine feeling

Arranged by Lorie Line

(Allow notes to sustain in each of the first three measures)

Joy To The World

Boldly

Arranged by Lorie Line

Marcato

As With Gladness

Quietly

Arranged by Lorie Line

Carol of the Bells

With bright, whirling motion

Arranged by Lorie Line

Revised from actual recording
for solo piano

Let melody sing

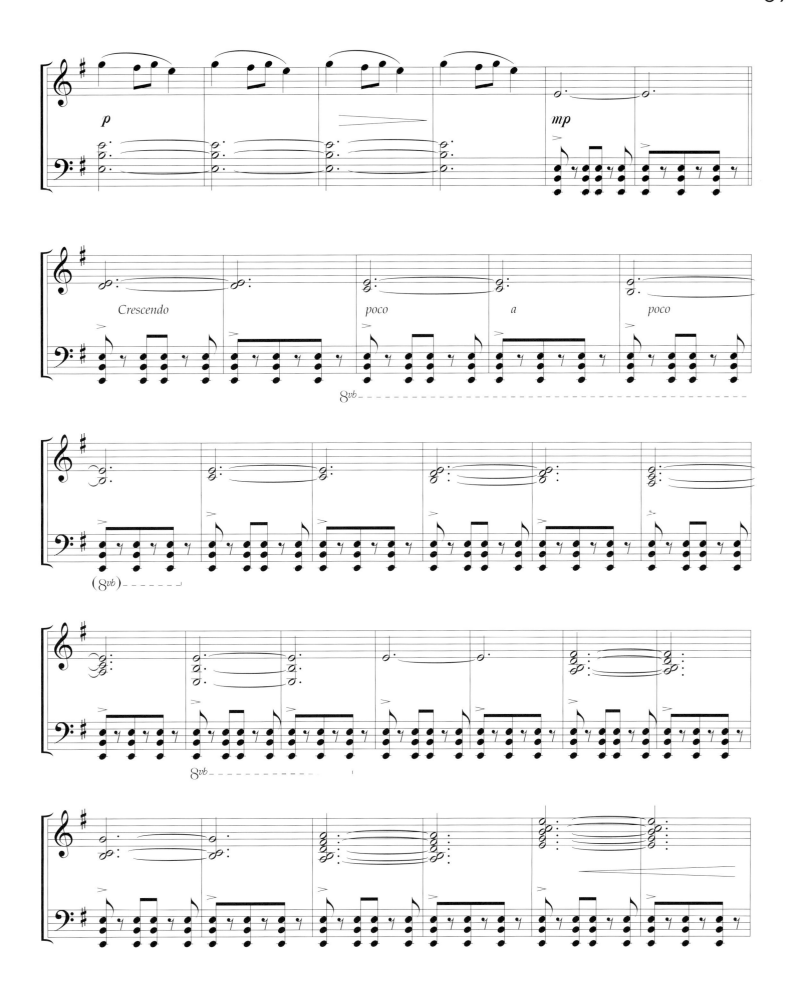

With driving intensity

Spanish Dance

Ave Maria

Serenely

Arranged by Lorie Line

The *Lorie Line* Music Collection

Young At Heart
The Classics, Volume I
Solo and Orchestrated Piano

The first volume in a series, this brand new release *Young At Heart* features great standards in a piano trio format. Performed with a small ensemble, each song reflects Lorie's personal piano style. The album includes great timeless favorites like *Misty, Autumn Leaves, Summertime, The Nearness of You, Smile, As Time Goes By, Young At Heart* (the title track), and many more.

Available in CD and Music Book.

Open House
Orchestrated Piano

Over one hour of intimate piano music, performed solo and with simple accompaniment featuring originals, Celtic and Irish music, traditionals and popular show tunes.

Available in CD and Music Book.

Best Seller!
Music from the Heart
Solo and Orchestrated Piano

Features 17 of the most requested contemporary standards from movies and Broadway in Lorie's recognizable style. This is a compilation of the best and most well-known songs.

Available in CD and Music Book.

Best Seller!
Threads of Love
Solo and Orchestrated Piano

Definitely Lorie's best selling album.

Available in CD and Sheet Music Singles.

Threads of Love
Rondo
From the Heart

Beyond A Dream
Solo and Orchestrated Piano

Some of the best cover tunes plus two original pieces from Lorie.

Available in CD and Sheet Music Single.

Beyond A Dream

Just Me
Solo Piano

This album combines the top two favorite areas of Lorie's music together—solo piano and all-original. *Just Me* features Lorie's own compositions without accompaniment in her very personal and heartwarming style. Features 14 original songs which are sure to be favorites.

Available in CD and Music Book.

Walking With You
Solo and Orchestrated Piano

A mixture of classic, popular and original tunes.

Available in CD and Music Book.

Heart and Soul
Orchestrated Piano

This is fully orchestrated and features visual melody lines that are memorable and heartwarming. This all-original album is a 1995 release, has been on the charts in "Billboard" magazine and it features members of Lorie's Pop Chamber Orchestra.

Available in CD and Music Book.

Simply Grand
Solo Piano

This one hour recording features some of the most romantic music of all time plus Lorie Line originals. *Simply Grand* reflects its title in the purest form—simple and grand. Fifteen songs.

Available in CD and Music Book.

Lorie Line Live! Best Seller!
Solo Piano Music Book

Eighty pages of solo piano music from Lorie's first national PBS television special. Features the most requested and popular music from Lorie and highlights from her popular original album, *Heart and Soul*. A Best Seller!

Available in Music Book only.

The Heritage Collection
Volume III
Orchestrated Piano

Features some of the most beloved historic American music, patriotic songs and classic and timeless hymns.
A fully orchestrated album, this music is very "fresh", emotionally moving and sometimes very exciting. Over one hour of music, 16 songs!

Available in CD and Music Book.

The Heritage Collection
Volume I
Solo and Orchestrated Piano

Uplifting songs and hymns from our heritage.

Available in CD and Music Book.

The Show Stoppers
Orchestrated Piano with Vocal Performance

Robert Robinson performs with Lorie Line & her Pop Chamber Orchestra. For 10 years Lorie Line has toured with her Pop Chamber Orchestra. In the makeup of this group has been a very special person, vocalist Robert Robinson. When he joined the tour in 1992, the show would never be the same. He had the gift to bring people to tears and to their feet, night after night. His voice literally stopped the show with applause every night in every city.

Available in CD only.

The Heritage Collection
Volume II
Solo and Orchestrated Piano

Sixteen timeless piano arrangements, featuring songs of inspiration. One hour of music.

Available in CD and Music Book.

The Big Band
Sharing The Season
Volume Four
Orchestrated Piano

This recording is the most fully orchestrated big band album ever recorded by Lorie & her Pop Chamber Orchestra. In high contrast to an intimate solo piano recording, this album is "big", high energy, and lots of fun! It reflects the personality of a live show. You will find your toes tapping and your fingers snapping when you listen to this music. Features over one hour of music, 16 songs!

Available in CD and Music Book.

Sharing The Season
Volume I
Solo and Orchestrated Piano

Features 15 classic and traditional holiday songs: *Silent Night, It Came Upon A Midnight Clear, Oh Come Little Children, Away In A Manger* and many more Christmas favorites.

Available in CD and Music Book.

Sharing The Season
Volume III
Orchestrated Piano

This holiday album features Lorie's upbeat material performed on her holiday tour. It is a joyous recording, showcasing unique styles and cultural influences. This is one of Lorie's personal favorite holiday albums and a best seller.

Available in CD and Music Book.

The Silver Album
Solo Piano Holiday Favorites

This is the first solo piano holiday album ever to be released by Lorie. The entire album is easy-listening and features 16 classics and favorites: *White Christmas, O Tannenbaum, Angels From The Realms Of Glory, Bells Over Bethlehem, The Christmas Song, Have A Holly Jolly Christmas* and more.

Available in CD and Music Book.

Sharing The Season
Volume II
Solo and Orchestrated Piano

If you're tired of the same ol' Christmas songs, this orchestrated piano album features traditional holiday songs, some of which may be new to you.

Available in CD and Music Book.

Best Seller!
Home For The Holidays
Solo Piano Music Book

Fifteen solo piano arrangements of Lorie's most popular holiday songs from her *Sharing The Season* albums. A Best Seller!

Available in Music Book only.